Supporting Dyslexic Learners in the Secondary Curriculum
Moira Thomson, MBE

DYSLEXIA:
ICT SUPPORT IN THE SECONDARY
CURRICULUM

First published in Great Britain by Dyslexia Scotland in 2007

Second edition for schools in England published in 2017 by CPD Bytes Ltd

ISBN 978-1-912146-30-7

This booklet is 1.6 in the series
Supporting Dyslexic Learners in the Secondary Curriculum (England)

Supporting Dyslexic Learners in the Secondary Curriculum   Moira Thomson, MBE

Complete set comprises 25 booklets

1.0   Dyslexia: Secondary Teachers' Guides

1.1   Identification and Assessment of Dyslexia at Secondary School

1.2   Dyslexia: Underpinning Skills for the Secondary Curriculum

1.3   Dyslexia: Reasonable Adjustments to Classroom Management

1.4   Dyslexia: Role of the Secondary School SENCo (Dyslexia Specialist Teacher)

1.5   Partnerships with Parents of Secondary School Students with Dyslexia

1.6   Dyslexia: ICT Support in the Secondary Curriculum

1.7   Dyslexia and Examinations (Reasonable Adjustments & Access Arrangements)

1.8   Dyslexia: Information for Guidance, Pastoral & Behaviour Support Teachers (2013)

1.9   Dyslexia: Learning Styles and Study Skills for the Secondary Curriculum NEW

1.10   Dyslexia: Role of the Teaching Assistant NEW

1.11   Dyslexia: Co-occurring & Overlapping Issues (Specific Learning Difficulties) NEW

2.0   Dyslexia: Subject Teachers' Guides

2.1   Dyslexia: Art & Design Subjects

2.2   Dyslexia: Drama (Performing Arts; Theatre Studies)

2.3   Dyslexia: English (Communication)

2.4   Dyslexia: Home Economics (Child Development; Food & Nutrition)

2.5   Dyslexia: ICT Subjects (Business Subjects; Computer Science)

2.6   Dyslexia: Mathematics (Statistics)

2.7   Dyslexia: Modern Foreign Languages

2.8   Dyslexia: Music

2.9   Dyslexia: Physical Education (Sports; Games; Dance)

2.10   Dyslexia: Science Subjects (Biology; Chemistry; General Science; Physics)

2.11   Dyslexia: Social Subjects (Economics; Geography; History; Citizenship Studies; Philosophy; Religious Studies)

2.12   Dyslexia: The Classics (Classical Greek; Latin; Classical Civilisations) (2013)

2.13   Dyslexia: Media Studies NEW

2.14   Dyslexia: Social Sciences (Anthropology; Archaeology; Humanities; Psychology; Sociology) NEW

Foreword by Dr Gavin Reid, formerly senior lecturer in the Department of Educational Studies, Moray House School of Education, University of Edinburgh. An experienced teacher, educational psychologist, university lecturer, researcher and author, he has made over 1000 conference and seminar presentations in more than 40 countries and has authored, co-authored and edited many books for teachers and parents.

ACKNOWLEDGEMENTS

Moira Thomson would like to thank the following for making possible the original publication of this important series of booklets:

✦ Dyslexia Scotland for supporting the publication and distribution of the original editions of these booklets

✦ The Royal Bank of Scotland for an education grant that funded Dyslexia Scotland's support

✦ Dr Gavin Reid for his encouragement over the years – and for writing the Foreword to these booklets

✦ Dr Jennie Guise of DysGuise Ltd for her support and professional advice

✦ The committee of Dyslexia Scotland South East for their support

✦ Alasdair Andrew for all his hard work and unfailing confidence

✦ Colleagues Maggie MacLardie and Janet Hodgson for helpful comments

✦ Cameron Halfpenny for proof reading and editing these booklets

✦ Current and former students, whose achievements make it all worthwhile

Moira Thomson MBE
2017

FOREWORD by Dr Gavin Reid

The Dyslexia booklets written by Moira Thomson have been widely circulated and highly appreciated by teachers throughout Scotland and beyond. I know they have also been used by teachers in a number of countries and this is testimony to the skills of Moira in putting together these booklets in the different subject areas of the secondary school curriculum.

It is therefore an additional privilege for me to be approached again by Moira to update this Foreword to the compendium of books developed by Moira in association with Dyslexia Scotland.

These updated guides are for all teachers - they contain information that will be directly relevant and directly impact on the practice of every teacher in every secondary school in the country. It is heartening to note that the guides again provide a very positive message to readers. The term Dyslexia is not exclusive to the challenges experienced by learners with dyslexia, but there is now a major thrust towards focussing on the strengths and particularly what they **can** do - and not what they 'can't do'. It is important to obtain a learning profile which can be shared with the student.

Moira encapsulates these points in these updated booklets. The focus is on supporting learners and helping them overcome the barriers to learning. At the same time it is important that learners with dyslexia, particularly in the secondary school develop responsibility for their own learning. The acquisition of self-sufficiency in learning and self-knowledge is an important aspect of acquiring efficient learning skills for students with dyslexia. It is this that will stand them in good stead as they approach important examinations and the transition to tertiary education and the workplace. For that reason these guides are extremely important and need to be available to all teachers. Moira ought to be congratulated in endeavouring to achieve this.

The breadth of coverage in these guides is colossal. Moira Thomson has met this immense task with professionalism and clarity of expression and the comprehensiveness of the guides in covering the breadth of the curriculum is commendable.

As well as including all secondary school subjects the guides also provide information on the crucial aspects of supporting students preparing for examinations, the use of information and communication technology, information for parents, details of the assessment process and the skills that underpin learning. It is important to consider the view that learners with dyslexia are first and foremost 'learners' and therefore it is important that their learning skills are developed fully. It is too easy to place the emphasis on developing literacy skills at the expense of other important aspects of learning. The guides will reinforce this crucial point that the learning skills of all students with dyslexia can be developed to a high level.

The guides do more than provide information on dyslexia; they are a staff development resource and one that can enlighten and educate all teachers in secondary schools. I feel certain they will continue to be warmly appreciated. The guides have already been widely appreciated by teachers and school management as well as parents and other professionals, but the real winners have been and will continue to be the **students** with dyslexia. It is they who will ultimately benefit and the guides will help them fulfil their potential and make learning a positive and successful school experience.

Dr Gavin Reid, April 2016

WHAT IS DYSLEXIA?

Dyslexia is widely recognised as a specific difficulty in learning to read.

Research shows that dyslexia may affect more than the ability to read, write and spell – and there is a growing body of research on these 'co-occurring' factors.

The Rose Report[1] identifies dyslexia as *'a developmental difficulty of language learning and cognition that primarily affects the skills involved in accurate and fluent word reading and spelling, characterised by difficulties in phonological awareness, verbal memory and verbal processing speed.'*

Dyslexia is a learning difficulty that primarily affects the skills involved in accurate and fluent word reading and spelling.

Characteristic features of dyslexia are difficulties in phonological awareness, verbal memory and verbal processing speed.

Dyslexia occurs across the range of intellectual abilities.

It is best thought of as a continuum, not a distinct category, and there are no clear cut-off points.

Co-occurring difficulties may be seen in aspects of language, motor co-ordination, mental calculation, concentration and personal organisation, but these are not, <u>by themselves,</u> markers of dyslexia.

A good indication of the severity and persistence of dyslexic difficulties can be gained by examining how the individual responds or has responded to well-founded intervention.

Rose Report page 10

Dyslexia exists in all cultures and across the range of abilities and socio-economic backgrounds. It is a hereditary, life-long, neuro-developmental condition. Unidentified, dyslexia is likely to result in low self-esteem, high stress, atypical behaviour, and low achievement.[2]

Estimates of the prevalence of dyslexia vary according to the definition adopted but research suggests that dyslexia may significantly affect the literacy attainment of between 4% and 10% of children.

---

[1] Rose, J (2009) *Identifying and Teaching Children and Young People with Dyslexia and Literacy Difficulties* DCFS Publications - independent report to the Secretary of State for Children, Schools & Families June 2009
http://webarchive.nationalarchives.gov.uk/20130401151715/http://www.education.gov.uk/publications/eOrderingDownload/00659-2009DOM-EN.pdf

[2] From Scottish Government working definition of dyslexia
http://www.gov.scot/Topics/Education/Schools/welfare/ASL/dyslexia

TEACHERS' RESPONSIBILITIES RE LEARNERS WITH DYSLEXIA

References: Part 6 of the Equality Act 2010; Part 3 of the Children and Families Act 2014

All children/young people are entitled to an appropriate education, one that is appropriate to their needs, promotes high standards and the fulfilment of potential - to enable them to:
- achieve their best
- become confident individuals living fulfilling lives, and
- make a successful transition into adulthood, whether into employment, further or higher education or training

SEND Code of Practice 0-25[3]

All schools have duties towards individual children and young people to identify and address their Special Educational Needs/Disability (SEND). Dyslexia that has a substantial, long-term, adverse impact on day-to-day learning may be both SEN and a disability.

Teachers' responsibilities for meeting the needs of dyslexic learners are the same as those for all students, and should include approaches that avoid unnecessary dependence on written text.

Teachers have a responsibility to provide a suitably differentiated subject curriculum, accessible to all learners, that provides each with the opportunity to develop and apply individual strengths – and to ensure that learners with SEND get the support they need to access this. Rose[4] suggests that all teachers should have 'core knowledge' of dyslexia characteristics – to help them to make adjustments to their practice that will prevent discrimination and substantial disadvantage.

The reasonable adjustments made by subject teachers in the classroom should be reflected in the arrangements made for examinations in the subject concerned.

For example – if a History teacher usually reads source materials aloud to the whole class – then - for dyslexic students in that class – the usual way of working with source materials is to have them read aloud. If a Science teacher usually permits a dyslexic student, who struggles with writing and spelling, to dictate - e.g. observations during an experiment - to a scribe or audio-recorder– this is evidence of the student's usual way of producing written work in that subject.

---

[3] SEND Code of Practice 0-25
https://www.gov.uk/government/uploads/system/uploads/attachment_data/file/398815/SEND_Code_of_Practice_January_2015.pdf
[4] Rose Report (2009) page 17

SUBJECT TEACHERS' GRADUATED APPROACH TO DYSLEXIA SUPPORT SHOULD INCLUDE:

- Recognition of and sensitivity to the range and diversity of the learning preferences and styles of all learners

- Awareness of the learning differences related to dyslexia that may cause difficulties within the subject curriculum

    o Acknowledgement of the very severe difficulties some dyslexic learners experience due to failure to master early stages of literacy and numeracy

    o Understanding that dyslexia is developmental in nature and that some students who coped with the early stages of literacy acquisition may begin to experience difficulties with higher order skills and processing issues in the secondary curriculum

- Selection or design of appropriate teaching and learning programmes that match the range of all abilities, within the curricular framework of the school

- Commitment to the need to reduce barriers to learning linked to the delivery of the curriculum as well as those due to the impact of dyslexia

- Acceptance that some learners with dyslexia may require additional support within the context of a subject and to consult with parents, colleagues and specialists (and the young person) to determine how best to provide this

- Willingness to ask for advice and support from the SENCo and/or specialist teacher if a dyslexic learner does not make the expected progress towards achieving outcomes identified in the SEN Support Plan

- Understanding that, while dyslexia is not linked to ability, able dyslexic learners may persistently underachieve

- Knowledge that many dyslexic learners use strategies such as misbehaviour or illness for coping with difficulties they do not necessarily understand themselves

- Taking account of the difficulties experienced by dyslexic learners when reviewing progress so that subject knowledge and ability are assessed fairly by making reasonable adjustments to arrangements for assessments (Access Arrangements) that reflect the additional support usually provided in the classroom

Dyslexic learners constantly meet barriers to learning across the curriculum and may become discouraged very quickly due to lack of initial success in subject classes. This may result in subject teachers assuming that they are inattentive or lazy, when they are actually working much harder than their classmates, but with little apparent effect.

TECHNOLOGY IN THE CLASSROOM

Information, communication, technology[5] is now firmly embedded in the curriculum at all stages. Frequent computer and internet use helps all students to gain the digital skills they need to become effective learners in the twenty first century.

Developing expertise in the use of technology results in increased self-confidence and self-esteem for dyslexic learners by providing a familiar, multi-sensory learning environment, using spell checkers, word processing, word banks, and predictive lexicons as well as digital recorders and calculators, enabling them to:

- develop skills to meet their needs in a mainstream classroom with little intervention
- overcome barriers such as slow or illegible writing and spelling issues
- see text on screen and hear this read aloud as often as they need
- plan written work before starting and edit/review this before printing
- demonstrate subject knowledge and ability at an appropriate level
- have the confidence to work independently

Some dyslexic learners may become skilled technology users even though they struggle to read the instructions provided with their devices. However, most websites, textbooks and printed material still rely heavily on text to convey information; so dyslexic readers may still be disadvantaged when these are used. Fortunately, aids like screen text readers and voice activated software for writing have already created opportunities for dyslexics to participate fully in learning activities.

Some dedicated software tools that help dyslexic learners are available on up to date computers when the operating system includes:

- screen magnification which enlarges text/diagram size
- settings to increase and decrease contrast, remove colour (switch to greyscale)
- text-to-speech options which allow the computer to read aloud text displayed - within word processors and on websites
- speech to text software enabling the user to speak directly into a word processor
- word completion and spell checking options that improve efficiency with writing and recording
- on-screen keyboards and sticky keys which allow greater flexibility for those who experience concentration issues

---

[5] Assistive technology (AT) is defined as "*any item, piece of equipment, or product system that is used to increase, maintain, or improve functional capabilities of individuals with disabilities*".

Some of the features that are part of computer operating systems may be more suited to the needs of dyslexic learners if they are integrated into software packages offering additional features; such as:

- **Text-to-speech software**: for users who prefer to have on screen text read out loud. This can usually read out web pages, worksheets or textbooks; but some versions cannot read out PDF documents, which are often used to ensure that a document's layout is not changed – so additional software may be needed.

- **Text prediction software**: (like 'predictive texting' on a phone) which helps to speed up writing. Many word processors also offer text prediction and word completion, but packages that offer spelling and grammar checking and allow users to create subject/personal word banks to support word completions and prediction will be of more help to dyslexic students.

- **Concept (mind) mapping software**: helps learners to structure, visualise and classify ideas and can help with problem solving, decision-making and writing. Additional software packages can display concept map information in alternative formats: e.g. as bulleted lists or paragraphs. Dyslexic students can use concept maps as revision aids, story boards for structuring essays and project planning.

- **Screen magnification software**: enlarges any chosen section of the computer screen display and is useful for dyslexic learners who also have visual stress issues.

A computer may be set up so that it is exactly what a dyslexic student needs. Once a student's personal profile has been set up, it can be saved, stored and available whenever the machine is used. If a school network is in place, dyslexic students could have a 'roaming' profile that follows them wherever they log onto a computer on that network.

Many of these access features are now being built into portable devices such as smart-phones and MP3 players. It is now possible to convert text to a spoken track that can be used on an MP3 player or smart-phone without having to purchase any additional software, making text accessible for dyslexics who prefer to have text read to them.

PORTABLE READING AND WRITING SUPPORT

There is a wide range of portable assistive technology available that can support dyslexic students with reading and writing difficulties. Hardware available ranges from tablet and laptops, Personal Digital Assistants (PDAs), scanners, spellcheckers and dictionaries.

LAPTOPS/NET-BOOKS/TABLETS

Laptop or net-book use in the classroom provides dyslexic students with opportunities for multi-sensory learning using touch, motion, vision and sound. Whether a laptop/net-book is issued by the school or provided by parents, these are easy to use in secondary classrooms and are often linked to the school network and Wi-Fi.

The **MacBook Air** and **iPad tablets** are already used in many classrooms and there are many apps available to make these even more dyslexia friendly. **Classroom** is a powerful new iPad app that helps teachers guide learning, share work and manage student devices.

The **iPad Pro** is the next generation of iPad tablet and is available as a 12.9 inch or 9.7 inch device. This lightweight, powerful computer has high quality colour and sound features, and uses fingerprint ID instead of passwords. The battery lasts for 10 hours so could be used throughout the school day. The **Apple Pencil** maybe used with the iPad Pro when greater precision and versatility is needed.

For many, a keyboard remains a convenient way to put thoughts down and get work done. **The Smart Keyboard** features innovative technologies without batteries, switches or plugs. The Smart Connector transfers both data and power between iPad Pro and the Smart Keyboard. No batteries or charging required; just attach the Smart Keyboard, and the onscreen keyboard disappears. Unlike traditional keyboards the keys have been laser ablated into a single sheet of durable fabric coated in a water- and stain-resistant finish. The keyboard does double duty by acting as a lightweight cover for the tablet, unfolding as required.

MOBILE PHONES/PDAS

Many mobile phones today are powerful, versatile computers. With the exception of the IPad, PDAs have been largely replaced by smart-phones - which can run web browsers, e-mail, e-book readers, audio recorders and educational tools – and have a zoom function that enlarges displays for ease of reading.

E-BOOK READERS

Most e-books can be read on a laptop or tablet computer, but there are some dedicated e-readers available which cost less and may have access to a wide range of 'free' e-books.

There are several versions of the **Kindle e-reader** available and not all have the full range of features, though all but the cheapest now have a text to speech app. Most Kindles will provide features that:

- adjust text size - a choice of up to eight text sizes offered

- show information about a book - *About This Book* shows background information about the author and the book

- look up unknown words - *Word Wise* shows short definitions above difficult words automatically, so dyslexic students can continue reading without interruption. Tapping on a word will call up a card showing definitions, synonyms and more

- review new vocabulary - words looked up are automatically added to *Vocabulary Builder* to expand knowledge and reinforce retention. Students can swipe through vocabulary words, do a quiz using flashcards, and see those words in context

- look up references without leaving the page - *Smart Lookup* integrates a dictionary with *X-Ray* and *Wikipedia* allowing access to definitions, characters, settings and more without leaving the page or losing the place

- explore the book - *X-Ray* shows all the passages in a book that mention relevant ideas, fictional characters, historical figures, places, or topics of interest. A timeline view makes it easy to review passages or navigate through images

- find the place - *Whispersync* technology synchronises the last page read across devices so it is easy to pick up exactly where you left off

- find out how long it will take to finish a chapter or book - *Time to Read* is personalised based on reading speed and is constantly updated as an individual's reading speed and habits change

DIGITAL VOICE RECORDERS

Students with dyslexia often

- have a slow handwriting speed
- find it difficult to write neatly
- get distracted when trying to think about a spelling
- have problems writing, copying or taking notes whilst listening
- struggle with recall when revising

The quality of the microphone and the rapid draining of the battery make tablets and phones impractical as recorders in the classroom. Digital Voice Recorders support dyslexic students in a range of tasks including

- making personal notes
- taking down homework and other tasks
- recording lessons, lectures and discussions
- listening to audio files created with text-to-speech software

The **Olympus DM-7 Digital Voice Recorder** has Wi-Fi smart-phone compatibility, a stereo sound microphone, and features Voice Command & Text-to-Speech Functions. The Olympus app which supports Remote Control and Visual Index is downloadable free of charge. Recorded files may be downloaded to a computer or smart-phone.

PORTABLE ELECTRONIC DICTIONARY AND THESAURUS

Using a traditional paper dictionary and thesaurus can be extremely difficult for dyslexic students. Even when target words are presented in different colours or highlighted, accessing alphabetic arrangement on pages of closely packed text in a very small font size may be beyond the search skills of many dyslexics and result in visual stress.

Portable electronic devices such as **Franklin Spell checkers and dictionaries** can alleviate these difficulties and provide comprehensive solutions for dyslexic students. Using a device like this reduces the strain on working memory experienced when using a paper dictionary.

READING PENS

Reading **PenWizzComTech** reading pens are hand-held literacy support tools used to boost vocabulary, phonemic awareness, fluency and comprehension for dyslexic students. A reading pen may enable the user to scan a word by running the pen over it. Depending on the pen, the user can then listen to the word and (possibly) the definition. This is most useful for those dyslexic students who experience <u>occasional</u> issues with subject vocabulary.

The **C-pen reader** is a small, lightweight device ideal for dyslexic students to use anywhere. It has an accurate optical character recognition (OCR) engine which enables the capture and instant saving of printed text. The pen is dragged across printed text and it instantly displays the word definition and reads it aloud using a British-English text-to-speech engine - allowing students to listen to pronunciations of words or listen to paragraphs of text read aloud. Using the integrated electronic dictionary, words can be scanned and the definition displayed. As well as a high-quality scanning device, the C-Pen Reader doubles up as a USB drive with 1GB of space available. (compatible with PC and Mac)

The C-Pen Exam Reader is a small, lightweight device and is half the size and weight of other portable pen scanners. This scanning device ideal for anyone who has dyslexia who has some reading issues that result in problems during exams. Students simply run the pen across printed exam text and instantly hear this read aloud. The Exam Reader has been approved by The Joint Council for Qualifications (JCQ) for use in exams - so students can take exams knowing that they can read and understand the questions – even in subjects where a human reader is not permitted.

ICT TO REMOVE BARRIERS TO LEARNING IN THE SUBJECT CLASSROOM

Visual Stress

Visual stress can range from blurred letters or words, headaches, or difficulty with tracking across a page. There is a wide range of assistive technology that can help with visual stress including coloured overlays which are placed over text to make reading more comfortable. There are also tools such as coloured paper, tinted reading rulers and software for use on computers or mobile devices.

BARRIERS TO LEARNING: VISUAL ISSUES:

- glare and reflected light on whiteboard
- visual issues including discomfort when reading
- distortions in text
- headaches or nausea when reading or writing at length

REASONABLE ADJUSTMENTS USING ICT:

- alter the format of interactive whiteboard displays and on computer screens; e.g. change background colour; font size, style and colour; line and paragraph spacing and use of zoom
- modify colours of screen backgrounds, text and menus to meet individual preferences

Dyslexic students who use coloured overlays when reading may benefit from using a virtual version on the computer screen: e.g. *Virtual Reading Ruler* (Crossbow Education).

BARRIERS TO LEARNING: READING ISSUES:

- dyslexic students reading rate and accuracy are often much slower than other students, causing them to fall behind the class in some subjects
- reading comprehension is sometimes poor, as dyslexic students have to concentrate on decoding text and have little working memory capacity left to process content

REASONABLE ADJUSTMENTS USING ICT:

- add speech support to existing programs, applications and web pages: e.g. a text to speech program to read text aloud
- scan subject course materials and texts into the computer and to be read aloud
- permit dyslexic students to use their own earbuds when using test to speech software

Text to speech programs are particularly useful when the text being spoken is highlighted simultaneously; supporting developing phonological processing skills as well as improving sight vocabulary.

IMPACT OF ICT USE: Dyslexic students are able to work more independently, in a non-threatening environment when:

- use of a computer screen reader enables dyslexic students to see and hear all text onscreen; supporting access to text material in most situations
- reading rate, fluency and comprehension are improved; e.g. the dyslexic student does not have to stop to decode unknown words or phrases
- dyslexic students have more working memory available to help speed up processing rate and improve reading comprehension
- self-esteem is improved when dyslexic students' differences are minimised; e.g. using barely visible earbuds

BARRIERS TO LEARNING: WRITING ISSUES: dyslexic students
- often have poorly formed handwriting that deteriorates over time
- tend to write only short summaries of subject knowledge because of issues with handwriting and spelling of subject vocabulary
- often have difficulty identifying errors in their own work – they see what they wanted to write rather than what is there
- may struggle to read poorly formed handwriting when reviewing their work
- have difficulty redrafting written work – often having to copy out the whole piece again (and probably make additional errors)
- hand in messy and difficult to read work – even when the content is correct

REASONABLE ADJUSTMENTS USING ICT:
Word processing is a key written communication tool used in schools. This enables dyslexic students to minimise the impact of their dyslexia on writing by:
- learning keyboarding skills to make the physical act of writing less stressful and tiring
- using subject vocabulary supported by word banks/spell checkers to remove errors
- using text to speech (screen reading) software to provide a spoken version of typed work so errors are more easily identified and content reviewed;
- redrafting written text more easily: text is moved around a page, using facilities such as delete, cut, copy and paste; or highlighted and dragged by more competent keyboard users

IMPACT OF ICT USE: dyslexic writers are able to write at greater length without the fear that their subject language is mis-spelled or incorrect. Self-esteem and confidence in their writing is improved as:
- using a computer keyboard is less stressful and tiring than handwriting, and good keyboarding skills support dyslexic processing issues, allowing thoughts to be written as they occur then re-ordered later
- dyslexic students may have the option of hearing typed text as it is entered allowing self-correction when writing
- reading back of typed work enables dyslexic students to review content, and check that they have used accurate subject vocabulary
- work is printed and handed in only when a final version is ready – so is always neat

SOFTWARE TO SUPPORT DYSLEXIC LEARNERS

There are many software packages available to support dyslexic learners and each has its own unique selling point or offers specific features that may help to overcome a particular reading or writing difficulty[6].

TYPING TUTORS

Learning to touch type brings many benefits to dyslexic individuals, reducing the need for handwriting, (often a disliked or problematic area), and typing is easily corrected without original mistakes being apparent; computer usage is more efficient and Spell Checkers provide invaluable help. Typing Tutors help individuals to type quickly and accurately when using a computer, which facilitates learning to spell, by making spelling more than a simple visual skill: spelling also becomes patterns on the keyboard, and patterns and spatial skills are often areas of strength for dyslexic students. Many of the tutors available are aimed at younger children – though some secondary students still enjoy the 'games' aspect of these.

Dance Mat Typing is an interactive game that has different levels and different stages so users learn how to touch type in a step-by-step manner. The game uses colourful cartoons that interact and communicate with the players and teaches how to use the letter keys, basic punctuation marks, and even how to capitalize words when touch typing. BBC Bitesize keyboarding tutor **Dance Mat** may be freely downloaded from http://www.kidztype.com/

Nessy Fingers is a typing tutor with a difference, using the alphabet to teach keyboard skills unlike other typing tutors that start with the 'home row'. There are several games to help improve keyboarding skills and a 'settings' menu allows different colour styles for the text bar and a range of sounds is available for the different games. A timer is available for the games and there is a 'Hall of Fame' complete with trophies as a reward for accurate typing.

Englishtype: at the same time as teaching typing, this software encourages reading, spelling, grammar & punctuation skills, using high frequency word lists and age-relevant and useful vocabulary. The software features:
- a multi-sensory approach
- choice of background screen colours
- unique key/finger colour coding
- visually simple presentation
- both written & spoken instructions
- tests of typing skill and awards for achievement
- an electronic diary to record practice

---

[6] See the B.D.A. New Technologies Committee resources: e.g. ICT Software to support literacy
https://bdatech.org/learning/i-c-t-for-literacy/

There are spelling lessons & vocabulary setting for dyslexic teens & adults and, unlike other typing tutors, lesson data is highly structured, e.g. non-words are controlled letter patterns only. (Available in junior or senior versions and for a PC or a Mac)

READING AND WRITING

There is a wide range of software available to help individuals with reading and writing difficulties covering spelling, grammar, vocabulary, literacy and phonics support. Some ICT tools will enable any text on screen to be heard – which may be a better solution for older dyslexic students, who wish to read a wider range of articles e.g. from the World Wide Web - or access texts from a scanner or word processor.

Text-to-speech Software

Text-to-speech software enables a computer to read aloud text documents, web pages, emails and PDF documents in a natural sounding voice. Most text-to-speech software now includes additional tools to support users including spell checkers and visual highlighting which support developing reading skills and help when producing written work.

AcceleRead AcceleWrite is a substantial electronic resource for teachers and parents, providing a teaching guide on how to use a computer with text-to-speech software to improve reading, writing, spelling and listening skills in students who are experiencing literacy difficulties. It contains colour-coded flash cards, record sheets and blank flash cards for individual use. This is now available as an app for iOS devices.[7]

ClaroRead is a simple, easy-to-use and flexible software program that helps with reading, writing, studying, and increases the dyslexic student's confidence. Any on-screen text can be out loud and writing in Microsoft Word improved. ClaroRead Plus and Pro also enables reading aloud of scanned paper books and documents with complete clarity.

TextHelp's **Browsealoud** software may be freely downloaded to add speech, reading, and translation to websites; facilitating access and participation for people with dyslexia. Online content can be read aloud in multiple languages using the most natural and engaging voice to transform the user's reading experience.

Their award-winning **Read&Write** is available for most computers and portable devices and gives students with dyslexia the confidence to access the web and read lengthy documents. A friendly, intuitive toolbar assists students at all levels with reading text, understanding unfamiliar words, researching assignments and proof reading written work.

For schools using Google Apps for Education, TextHelp's **Fluency Tutor** makes reading aloud more fun and satisfying for students who need some extra support. This easy to use app allows students to record themselves reading and then share that content with their teacher - away from the pressures of reading aloud in the classroom environment.

---

[7] www.dyslexic.com/apps

Speechstream is a flexible, cloud based, language and literacy support toolbar offering support functions to help improve student performance by making online courseware and learning systems more accessible. Reading, writing and maths support functions include:

- vocabulary list builder
- talking and picture dictionaries
- text-to-speech in multiple languages
- accurate read aloud of complex maths equations
- study skills annotation tools

Crick's **Clicker** software has been used for a number of years in primary schools and may continue to support the writing of dyslexic students in the early stages of secondary school, as teachers provide grids of words, phrases or pictures related to a particular lesson or learning objective. Features in Clicker 7, to encourage writing independence include:

- a word processer with built-in support tools
- child-friendly planning space (Clicker Board planning tool)
- an audio note taker
- realistic speech feedback
- word prediction (help with spelling and vocabulary)
- sentence building grids (help with words and phrases to help formulate sentences)

Speech Recognition

Speech recognition software allows individuals to transform spoken words into digital text, enabling them to create and edit documents, surf the web or send email, just by speaking. Some speech recognition software is up to 3 times faster than typing.

Improving accessibility through text-to-speech extends well beyond computer screens and mobile devices. Providing all students with equal access to learning materials is one of the core concepts of accessible education, and differentiated instruction.

LITERACY SUPPORT

Word processors now support literacy in a variety of ways – from checking that individual words are correctly spelled to checking grammar and punctuation to offering vocabulary suggestions from work banks – often offering the option of hearing words spoken to help selection.

Much of the literacy software available offers games or activities to practise skills in reading high frequency words, phonics and spelling - often using selected lists or a structured program aimed at different age/stage students – many suitable for primary age learners.

Wordshark provides word lists to use with over 40 motivating games to help reading, phonics, spelling and alphabetical order. The lists include subject vocabulary lists for KS3 and it is possible for subject teachers to add their own word lists. Detailed records are kept and certain activities can be printed onto worksheets for homework. Wordshark is available on USB pens for PC or Mac.

Electronic or interactive talking books

There are now many available both fiction and non-fiction. Most have in built digital recordings but some can be used with Microsoft Speech or similar tools - and many texts of fiction and textbooks have been made available in electronic format. Schools and educational establishments can access hundreds of titles for their pupils to access from Load2Learn.

Talking books allow dyslexic students to read text in a supported environment and at a pace that suits their needs. These will usually highlight text as it is being spoken, in words or phrases and allow users to click on any word or phrase to hear it spoken. Some will explain tricky or technical vocabulary. Many dedicated talking books to support reading offer options to alter format (colour, font, size, line spacing and background).

STUDY SKILLS

Planning for essays and assignments is very often linked to the use of lesson notes and concept or mind mapping when ideas are generated in a graphical way. Not all dyslexic students enjoy the use of concept mapping. Some prefer the structure of lists and outlines in notes with bullet points and numbers - though some mapping tools include this feature.

Note-taking

There is a wide range of note-taking support technology to help eliminate the difficulties that are associated with writing whilst listening. Many dyslexic students now make recordings of classroom talks and instructions for reference and revision, but do not make notes from them. Some new software helps with organising and editing recorded notes.

Audio Note-taker (Sonocent) offers a visual and interactive form of note-taking –where audio, text and images are used to create truly comprehensive notes. The software includes the option to split notes into more manageable chunks using track marks from the audio files and displays them on screen as a bar. These may be organised by colour coding and annotating them. PowerPoint or PDF slides may be imported to create comprehensive and meaningful notes.

Note-talker Edit for Windows is assistive technology software designed to use with the Note-talker app for phones and tablets. This may support dyslexic users with note-taking during lessons. Recordings can be uploaded to Note-talker Edit using Dropbox, iCloud or GoogleDrive where bookmark tags, PowerPoint slides and images can be loaded to add to notes. Note-talker Edit can be used with a digital voice recorder and desktop software.

CONCEPT MAPPING

Concept mapping (mind mapping) is an established learning and organisational tool, which enables dyslexic students to get their thoughts and ideas down in a structured way, to create maps and diagrams to represent their ideas. It can be used in different subject areas and for a range of tasks.

Many dyslexic students may have worked with **Kidspiration** at primary school. **Inspiration 9** mind mapping software provides older students with a framework for thinking. It can be used for visual mapping, outlining, writing and making presentations by providing a platform to organise help ideas.

- *Diagram* and *Map Views* help dyslexics to structure thoughts
- *Thinking* and *Planning* help to encourage creativity and confidence
- *Presentation Manager* enables diagrams, mind maps and outlines to be transformed into presentations

Creating mind maps is very easy, and a wide range of templates from different subjects is provided. A mind/concept map can be transformed into an outline at the click of a button enabling planning and organisation of written work. (Windows and Mac compatible)

MEMORY

Mastering Memory software encourages 'thinking' about memory as a process, providing a way to externalise this and review attitudes, techniques and strategies that can help in real life situations, allowing students to gain an understanding of their own memories.

Timely Reminders is software that helps students to remember facts and information by:

- helping students to organise the reinforcement and revision of any information so that it is transferred into automatic long-term memory
- helping students to recall the facts automatically and efficiently

MATHS/NUMBER

Literacy has always been the first priority for dyslexic learners, but numeracy and maths - involving memory, sequencing, direction, vocabulary and problem solving strategies, as well as calculations - may also be affected.

Number Shark uses colourful graphics in structured learning tasks and games. It covers the four main rules of numbers as well as decimals, fractions and percentages, giving users the chance to build up confidence, and the opportunity to practise those aspects of numbers that worry them, in an enjoyable way.

Dynamo Maths is a three-stage online intervention programme for learners who experience difficulties with maths. Using games, activities and printed resources, designed specifically to develop mental strategies and confidence, learners are encouraged to learn maths using a multi-sensory approach.

FURTHER READING

British Assistive Technology Association *Raising Awareness of Assistive Technology* http://www.bataonline.org/

British Dyslexia Association *Technology support for all dyslexic people* https://bdatech.org/

Cochrane, K & Saunders, K (editors) (2012) *Dyslexia Friendly Schools Good Practice Guide* Bracknell, British Dyslexia Association Ch. 11

Coogan, J & Flecker, M (2003) *Dyslexia in Secondary School: A Practical Handbook for Teachers, Parents and Students* London, Whurr Ch. 3

Hawes, B (2015) *Getting It right for Dyslexic Learners: The complete teachers' toolkit* Stafford, Crossbow Education Ltd.

Keates, A (2002) *Dyslexia and Information and Communications Technology, a Guide for Teachers and Parents* (2nd Edition) London, David Fulton Publishers

MacKay, N (2005) *Removing Dyslexia as a Barrier to Achievement: The Dyslexia Friendly Schools Toolkit* 3rd Edition (2012) Wakefield, SEN Marketing

Nuttal, J & Nuttal, L (2013) *Dyslexia and the iPad: Overcoming Dyslexia with Technology* CreateSpace Independent Publishing Platform

Smythe, I (2010) *Dyslexia in the Digital Age* London, Continuum International Publishing Group

Thomson, M (2007) *Supporting Students with Dyslexia at Secondary School – every class teacher's guide to removing barriers and raising attainment* London, Routledge Ch. 9

LAPTOP USE BY DYSLEXIC STUDENTS IN THE SECONDARY CLASSROOM
A Practical Guide for Subject Teachers (PHOTOCOPIABLE)

Subject teachers should have clear rules for student use of ICT in their classroom. In some subjects, every student is encouraged to use a laptop, net-book or tablet; but some rooms may not accommodate this, so the class should know that dyslexic students have priority.

Teachers should be prepared:
- make sure that laptop users sit near power points to avoid dead batteries
- beware of trailing cables – issue safety rules
- check that students' desks are big enough – laptop use may need 2 desks together
- arrange printing details in advance
- arrange for laptops to be set up at the start of the lesson to avoid later distractions
- make sure that dyslexic students can load a subject notes template easily
- ensure that class work is labelled at the start of the lesson and saved regularly
- if a planned lesson involves drawing diagrams, discuss this in advance with the student: e.g. do by hand and scan; draw onto the screen etc.
- if a lesson requires tables to be completed, make sure there is a template available
- if the student has screen reading software, keep a spare headset available
- insist that all sound effects are turned off when no headset is used
- arrange how homework will reach you: e.g. e-mail; saved on school network in prearranged file; printed and handed in etc.

Teachers need to decide:
- when a lesson will not be suitable for laptop use and warn students in advance
- how subject work is set out; give students an instruction sheet to follow at first
- how completed work is to be stored; filed electronically or as hard copy.

Dyslexic students should be encouraged to:
- use the laptop for all writing and reading if a text reader is used
- sit correctly – both feet on the floor, back straight, hands on the keyboard etc.
- take proper care of the laptop and have a routine for dealing with it as hardware
- elaborate on text later – adding various features not part of the standard layout
- organise all work in properly labelled folders.

Teachers should be alert for:
- students' love of strange fonts, bold text and odd colour designs; set rules for these
- students' greater concentration on the laptop than on lesson content
- 'technical' excuses for incomplete or 'lost' work
- Laptop screens being seen by other students in tests; so arrange seating to prevent this.

PREPARING A DOCUMENT FOR TEXT-READING SOFTWARE

Reading a document using a text reader will take longer than visual reading, so teachers should take account of this when planning reading activities.

Following these rules will ensure that text material is read aloud accurately – and more understandably - by the screen reader:

1. **CONTENTS LIST/MENU:**
    - number menu items
    - use hyperlinks (internal and external) to aid navigation

2. **TEXT:**
The computer software that generates the voice used for reading aloud will sound less 'artificial' if the writer:
    - uses a pale text colour similar to the background colour to make additional punctuation marks less visually distracting for the student
    - puts full stops after headings to create a pause
    - use semi-colons, commas, or full stops after bullet points in order to separate each point
    - do not use block capital letters in the middle of text: these may be read as single letters
    - use only the signs and symbols that are absolutely necessary to make sense of the text
    - avoid using dashes: e.g. a dash will be read as "dash" not used for a pause
    - colons can be used to make the voice pause
    - hyphens could be used between syllables in compound words to aid text reading pronunciation: e.g. dis-allow
    - Use straight double quotation marks only; not single slanted marks
    - when using abbreviations and acronyms full stops maybe needed
    - if a picture or image contains text, it may not be read aloud; this should be repeated in the main text.

3. **NUMBERS, SYMBOLS AND TABLES:**
Screen readers may be unable to read information presented in tables. They may not read the information in the required order; or they may not move on to the next cell automatically without manual use of the Tab key.
    - do not use Roman numerals or the abbreviation No. when numbering items
    - chunk phone numbers to avoid being read as millions or hundreds of thousands

ICT USE FOR EXAMS (PHOTOCOPIABLE)

The use of ICT must not compromise the validity of the assessment. The arrangements for the use of ICT in an assessment should reflect the candidate's usual way of working in the subject classroom.

Speech recognition technology and other specified software may be used only by those who have permission to use a scribe; and scribes may type responses for these candidates.

The JCQ's requirements for using ICT in external exams must be met:
- a word processor is used as a type-writer, not as a database
- standard formatting software is acceptable - but spell-checks and predictive software must be disabled, unless specifically approved
- candidates cannot access any other electronic sources[8]
- an auto-save facility is available (where possible)
- any memory stick provided should be cleared of any previously stored data
- separate accommodation provided if ICT use is likely to distract other candidates[9]
- contingency arrangements are in place to deal with any technical problems
- the candidate's word-processed work is printed out (as explained below)
- any additional or graphical work produced by the candidate is attached and submitted in the normal way

PRINTING
After the exam is over, the computer must be connected to a printer so that a script can be printed, or a portable storage medium – e.g. a memory stick cleared of other data before use – connected to a printer. Candidates must be present to verify that work printed is their own and that scripts are attached to any answer booklet which contains some answers.

USE OF A COMPUTER READER
A computer reader may be used in exams is this is the candidate's normal way of reading - **even in exams when a reader is not permitted** such as for the Reading component of an English exam or an MFL reading paper – because:
- A human reader can add a layer of vocal interpretation (nuance and meaning) which could affect a candidate's response and therefore compromise the reliability of the qualification.
- A computer reader allows a candidate to meet the requirements of the reading standards independently because the computer reader and a human reader do not interpret text in the same way.

---

[8] including the internet, locally-stored files, network shares, thumb drives, CDs, DVDs, e-mail and instant messaging systems, or any other digital media sources that are accessible either locally or over a wired or wireless network
[9] the need for additional invigilation must be taken into account

ACCESS ARRANGMENTS: DIGITAL QUESTION PAPERS (PHOTOCOPIABLE)

Digital question papers are an Access arrangement available to dyslexic candidates (and others who have SEND) where the actual exam paper is provided in digital format: and may even be online.

Using digital question papers will reflect the usual way of working for those students who habitually use computer screen readers and word processors in the classroom. Even if a digital paper is not available for a subject, a computer screen reader and a word processor may be permitted.

A digital question paper or computer screen reader may be permitted in subjects where a human reader is not allowed. But extensive practice must be arranged to ensure that this has become the candidate's usual way of working when a human reader is not available.

A digital question paper displays the question paper on-screen, enabling candidates to:
- change the colour of the display – background or text
- change the size of the displayed paper
- read the question paper on screen using text-to-speech software
- type/dictate responses on screen

The digital format is not suitable for all subjects:
- Subject exams where straightforward text answers are required are most suited
- Maths and science subjects contain subject-specific formulae and require answers in the form of figures, formulae or drawings: so a screen reader may not work well
- Sometimes question papers contain an objective test (multiple-choice) which can be read by a computer screen reader, though the answer grid must be filled in by hand

Using a computer in an exam requires not only familiarity with the keyboard and basic commands, but also with the software and the toolbars provided. Students may experience additional difficulties rather than gain access to an exam paper if they are not accustomed to e.g. the version of screen reader provided in the exam. When written work is also done on the computer, the exam centre should ensure that, where possible, an auto save facility is available and that the candidate is experienced in its use.

Prior to the exam, the school must ensure that the computer (or tablet if permitted):
- is cleared of any stored data
- cannot access unauthorised files or applications stored on the tablet, internet or other electronic devices
- Wi-Fi and Bluetooth settings are turned off

At the end of the exam time, completed and saved work is printed by the member of staff providing technical support supervised by the invigilator, with the candidate present.